W9-CDM-990

Exploring World Cultures

Austria

By Kaitlin Scirri

Cavendish
Square

New York

Published in 2022 by Cavendish Square Publishing, LLC
243 5th Avenue, Suite 136, New York, NY 10016

Website: cavendishsq.com

This publication represents the opinions and views of the author based on his or her personal experience, knowledge, and research. The information in this book serves as a general guide only. The author and publisher have used their best efforts in preparing this book and disclaim liability rising directly or indirectly from the use and application of this book.

All websites were available and accurate when this book was sent to press.

Library of Congress Cataloging-in-Publication Data

Names: Scirri, Kaitlin, author.
Title: Austria / Kaitlin Scirri.
Description: First Edition. | New York : Cavendish Square Publishing, 2022.
| Series: Exploring world cultures | Includes index.
Identifiers: LCCN 2020036433 | ISBN 9781502658968 (Library Binding) | ISBN
9781502658944 (Paperback) | ISBN 9781502658951 (Set) | ISBN
9781502658975 (eBook)
Subjects: LCSH: Austria--Juvenile literature. | Austria--Description and
travel. | Austria--History--Juvenile literature. | Austria--Social life
and customs.
Classification: LCC DB17 .S38 2022 | DDC 943.6--dc23
LC record available at https://lccn.loc.gov/2020036433

Editor: Katie Kawa
Copy Editor: Nicole Horning
Designer: Jessica Nevins

The photographs in this book are used by permission and through the courtesy of: Cover, pp. 16, 27 amriphoto/E+/Getty Images; p. 4 svetikd/E+/Getty Images; p. 5 CHUNYIP WONG/E+/Getty Images; p. 6 kosmozoo/DigitalVision Vectors/Getty Images; p. 7 borchee/E+/Getty Images; p. 8 Print Collector/Getty Images; p. 9 TASS via Getty Images; p. 10 Sylvain Sonnet/DigitalVision/Getty Images; p. 11 phototiger/E+/Getty Images; p. 12 praetorianphoto/E+/Getty Images; p. 13 Alex Gottschalk/DeFodi Images via Getty Images; p. 14 Ratnakorn Piyasirisorost/Moment/Getty Images; p. 15 ALEX HALADA/AFP via Getty Images; pp. 17, 21 DaveLongMedia/E+/Getty Images; p. 18 Albert Ceolan/De Agostini Picture Library via Getty Images; p. 19 Westend61/Brand X Pictures/Getty Images; p. 20 Laszlo Szirtesi/Getty Images; p. 22 Pierre Crom/Getty Images; p. 23 Kypros/Moment/Getty Images; p. 24 Bob Krist/The Image Bank Unreleased/Getty Images; p. 25 JOE KLAMAR/AFP via Getty Images; p. 26 HERBERT NEUBAUER/APA/AFP via Getty Images; p. 28 Peter Zelei Images/Moment/Getty Images; p. 29 GMVozd/E+/Getty Images.

Some of the images in this book illustrate individuals who are models. The depictions do not imply actual situations or events.

CPSIA compliance information: Batch #CS22CSQ: For further information contact Cavendish Square Publishing LLC, New York, New York, at 1-877-980-4450.

Printed in the United States of America

Find us on

Contents

Austria is a country in Central Europe. For many years, it was part of the Austro-Hungarian Empire, which was also known as Austria-Hungary. Today,

Many Austrians were born in Austria. Others came from different countries.

Austria and Hungary are two different countries.

In 1955, Austria was recognized as the modern independent nation it is today. Austria has nine states. Its capital city is Vienna (also known as Wien). Vienna also makes up the smallest state in Austria in terms of its area, but it has the largest population.

People from Austria are called Austrians. They speak Austrian German. It's a language similar to the German language spoken in Germany. Austrians share their country with many visitors from Europe and all over the world. Many travel

The Alps are the tallest mountains in Europe.

to Austria for its natural beauty. The Alps are a mountain range in Austria that **attract** people who enjoy skiing, snowboarding, hiking, and mountain climbing.

Austrians lead an active lifestyle. They enjoy sports, **festivals**, and the arts. They also know how to take it easy!

5

Austria isn't a large country. It's close to the size of the U.S. state of South Carolina, covering about 32,382 square miles (83,871 square kilometers). Austria is

This map of Austria shows its states (or provinces), its major cities, and its neighboring countries.

landlocked, which means it doesn't border any oceans. It borders eight other countries. Its longest border is the one it shares with Germany.

Northern and eastern Austria are mostly flat. The Alps reach across many parts of western

FACT!

The Danube is Austria's longest river and Europe's second longest river. It flows through 10 countries.

and southern Austria. The mountains are often covered in snow from November until May. Winters can be very cold in some parts of Austria, but summer days can reach

Lakes and rivers are found throughout Austria.

temperatures of 86 degrees Fahrenheit (30 degrees Celsius) or higher. Precipitation—rain in summer and snow in winter—falls evenly throughout the year.

Austria's Animals

Austria's wild animals include brown bears, rabbits, and deer. The country also hosts many birds, such as buzzards, owls, falcons, eagles, cranes, and swans. Austria's rivers are home to trout, pike, perch, and carp.

People have lived in what's now Austria for thousands of years. Both the **Celts** and the Romans ruled this land in its early history. In 976 CE, a noble family from Bavaria in what's now

Austria-Hungary was on the losing side of World War I, which began in 1914.

Germany took over the area. They were known as the Babenbergs. Later, another German family— the House of Habsburg—controlled Austria.

In 1867, this land became part of Austria-Hungary. After World War I ended in 1918,

The Austrian National Day is October 26. It's a day to celebrate, or honor, Austria's independence and neutrality.

Austria's First President

Karl Seitz was born in Vienna in 1869. He was president of Austria from 1919 to 1920. After being president, he was mayor of Vienna from 1923 to 1934.

Austria-Hungary broke apart. However, 20 years later, Austria was **invaded** by Germany. Germany controlled Austria throughout World War II (1939–1945). Ten years after the war, in 1955,

World War II left Austria broken. Austrians didn't want to be part of any more wars. They formally announced their neutrality, which meant they wouldn't take part in other countries' wars.

the Austrian State Treaty was signed. This meant that no other countries could have a presence in Austria. The country was now independent.

VOTE ✓

The Republic of Austria is a democratic republic. This means Austria's citizens vote to elect their leaders. Citizens can vote once they turn 16 years old.

Austria's parliament meets in this building in Vienna.

Austria's parliament passes new laws for the country. Parliament is made up of the National Council and the Federal Council. There are 183 members of the National Council. The size of the Federal Council is based on population and may change over time. In 2020,

FACT!

The judicial branch of Austria's government is made up of a system of courts.

The Constitution

Austria's constitution was adopted on October 1, 1920. It was revised, or changed, in small ways in 1929. The constitution set up the government and laid out the laws of the land.

the Federal Council had 61 members.

Austria has a president, who serves as its head of state. This means the president **represents** Austria to

The Austrian flag is red and white.

the rest of the world. The president also names a chancellor to oversee Austria's government. In 2019, Brigitte Bierlein was named Austria's first female chancellor.

Austria has a strong economy, or system of making, buying, and selling goods. Service is the top industry, or business, in Austria. Service jobs include

Austria has a lot to offer visitors, including beautiful cities such as Vienna.

teaching, nursing, and housekeeping. Tourism—the business of drawing in travelers—provides many jobs for Austrians. Many Austrians work in hotels, restaurants, ski resorts, and stores that are visited by tourists.

Germans make up the highest number of visitors to Austria.

The Euro

Austrian money is called the euro. It's used by many countries in the European Union (EU)— a group of countries in Europe that work together to deal with the economy, the natural world, and more.

Other Austrians work with machinery, metals, and cars. A small number of Austrians work in agriculture, or farming. Austrian farms produce grains, potatoes, fruit, dairy products, and grapes for wine. Some farmers also raise cattle, pigs, and chickens.

Many members of the EU, including Austria, use the same money, which is shown here.

Germany is Austria's top trading partner. The two countries trade goods such as machine parts and food.

Austria is known for its natural beauty. It has many rivers and lakes. There are also large areas of woods and meadows. Forests filled with spruce and other kinds of trees are found throughout the country.

Austria is rich in natural resources, or things found in nature that are valuable to people.

Austria is working hard to protect its forests, keeping the plants and animals in them safe.

FACT!

Austria gets some of its energy, or power, from fossil fuels such as oil and natural gas. However, Austria also gets energy from moving water.

Climate Change

Climate change is causing hotter temperatures and less snow in the Alps. Austria depends heavily on the Alps for its economy, so it's working to fight climate change by reducing air pollution.

Pollution has been a problem in Austria. However, rules are now in place to limit air pollution from factories and water pollution. Austrian farmers are also looking for ways

Austrian farmers play an important part in protecting the environment.

to help the environment, or natural world. Many farms in Austria are organic, which means they work with nature and not against it. For example, organic farmers don't use chemicals to kill pests or to help their plants grow.

15

Austria is home to almost 9 million people. People of Austrian **ancestry** make up most of the population. However, not everyone living in Austria was born there. Many

Austrian families love to have fun together!

people have come to Austria from other countries, such as Germany, Turkey, Serbia, and Romania.

Most people living in Austria are between 25 and 54 years old. The second largest age group is those who are 65 and older. There are more

FACT!

The most populated city in Austria is Vienna. Nearly 2 million people live there.

Fashion

Austrians most often dress in modern clothing such as jeans and sneakers. However, for festivals and special events, they often wear **traditional** Austrian clothing. A dirndl is a traditional dress for women. Lederhosen is a traditional pair of pants for men.

women than men living in Austria. Men in Austria live to an average age of 79. Women live to an average age of 85.

Some Austrians wear traditional clothing, such as the clothing shown here, for special events.

Families in Austria are small when compared to other countries in the world. Most Austrian families have only one or two kids.

Lifestyle

Some Austrians live in rural, or country, areas. However, most people live in urban areas such as towns and cities. They live near schools, offices, stores, and restaurants. People use many kinds of transportation, or ways of getting around, in Austria. Cars, buses, and trains are all common ways Austrians travel from one place to another.

Most Austrians have cell phones. They use

Trains can take people from Austria's mountains to its cities.

FACT!

Austrians love to go on vacation! They get at least five weeks of paid time off from work each year.

18

the internet for fun and to learn about what's going on in the world, just like people in many other countries. Many Austrians also use the internet to watch TV instead of more traditional methods.

Austrians like to spend time outdoors doing activities such as skiing and hiking.

Staying healthy is another important part of life in Austria. Austria has a good public health-care system, and individuals can pay for private care too.

Schools in Austria

Children in Austria are required to go to school from age 6 until age 15. At age 15, children may choose to stay in school or begin job training. Those who choose job training train until age 18.

Religion

People living in Austria may practice any religion, or belief system, they choose. Austrians also have the right not to practice any religion.

St. Stephen's Cathedral in Vienna is a Catholic church that dates back to the 12th century.

The main religion in Austria is Roman Catholicism. More than half of all Austrians belong to this branch of the Christian religion, which follows the teachings of Jesus Christ. Christian holidays, such as Christmas and Easter, are

FACT!

Buddhism became an official religion in Austria in 1983. This religion has its roots in Asia and comes from the teachings of a man known as the Buddha.

celebrated throughout the country.

A small percentage of Austrians practice Islam, which is based on the teachings of Muhammad. Muslims, or people who practice Islam, gather to pray in holy buildings called mosques.

Shown here is the inside of the church at St. Peter's Abbey in the city of Salzburg. Parts of the movie *The Sound of Music* were filmed at the abbey!

Jewish People in Austria

Austria was once home to large Jewish population. However, many Jewish people in Austria were killed during World War II. Today, the Jewish community in Austria is much smaller than it used to be.

Language

The official language of Austria is German. It's often called Austrian German or Austrian Standard German (ASG). Some words are spelled and pronounced, or said, differently in Austrian

Austrians often get their news from newspapers, such as these, printed in Austrian German.

German than they are in the German language spoken in Germany. However, most Germans and Austrians can understand each other.

FACT!

A common phrase in Austrian German is "auf Wiedersehen." It means "goodbye" or "see you again."

Regional Languages

Certain regions, or areas, in Austria have their own official minority languages. Croatian and Hungarian are minority languages in the state of Burgenland. Slovene is used in the state of Carinthia.

Almost 90 percent of the people living in Austria speak German. Austrian students are taught in German. It's the language used in newspapers, TV shows, and official

If you're driving on an Austrian road such as this one, it's important to know Austrian German!

government statements and reports.

Other languages spoken in Austria include Turkish, Serbian, and Croatian. Many Austrians also know English. It's often taught as a second language in Austrian schools.

Arts and Festivals

Austrians love music and hold many music festivals each year. Most festivals take place during the summer months of July and August. Many of the festivals are held outdoors. Some festivals last for days. Others, such as the

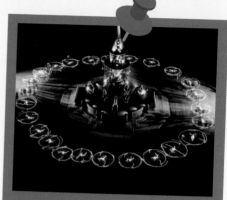

The Salzburg Festival opens with a special dance in which people carry torches, or fire.

Vienna Festival and the Salzburg Festival, last for weeks. These festivals celebrate music and other forms of art, including plays.

The celebrating doesn't stop when the

FACT!

The MuseumsQuartier Wien in Vienna is made up of several buildings for music, fashion, dance, and many other arts.

summer ends! Christmas is an important winter holiday in Austria. People come from all over Europe to enjoy Austria's Christmas markets in

The Christmas season is a beautiful time to visit Austria.

November and December. The markets offer treats such as gingerbread and holiday punch. Visitors can also buy gifts, including nutcrackers, ornaments, and other handcrafted goods.

The Music of Mozart

Wolfgang Amadeus Mozart was a famous Austrian classical musician. He was born in Salzburg in 1756, and he died in 1791. Today, Mozart is considered one of the greatest musicians and composers in history.

Rugby, soccer, and ice hockey are popular sports in Austria. Rugby is a sport that's similar to American football and is growing in popularity in Austria. However, it's

Shown here are members of Austria's national soccer team celebrating a goal.

still not as popular as soccer. Austria has many soccer teams, which are known as football teams in most countries outside the United States. Austria also has both men and women's ice hockey teams.

FACT!

Austrians have won more Olympic medals in Alpine, or downhill, skiing than people from any other country!

26

Shopping in Austria

Austrians love to shop! Cities such as Vienna have streets filled with fancy stores, but there are also many outdoor markets throughout the country.

Austria offers many outdoor activities, such as mountain climbing and hiking, that can be done all year. In addition, swimming, bicycling, and horseback riding are

Families in Austria often like to ski together.

popular in the summer. Austria's cold winters allow for ice-skating at outdoor rinks and skiing and snowboarding in the Alps.

Food

Food is an important part of life for people in every country, including Austria. Austrians love breakfast. Popular breakfast foods include rolls, pastries, cakes, and

Austrians like to drink coffee at home and in cafés with friends.

jam. Sometimes eggs, ham, and cheese are eaten for breakfast too. Coffee is very popular in Austria, and it's often served with hot, foamy milk on top. It sometimes has chocolate sprinkled on top too!

Austrians eat different kinds of meats,

One of Austria's most famous dishes is Wiener schnitzel, which is a thin piece of veal that's covered in breading and fried.

For a quick lunch or a snack, many Austrians visit a Wuerstelstand. It's similar to a hot dog stand. These stands serve sausages that are made quickly and don't cost a lot of money.

including roast beef, pork, veal, and sausages. Sausages are served many ways. Sometimes they're filled with cheese. Other times they might be served on a roll with

Tourists in Austria love trying Wiener schnitzel in the country that made it famous.

mustard and horseradish, similar to a hot dog.

Apple strudel is a popular dessert in Austria. It's a pastry filled with apples, raisins, nuts, and breadcrumbs.

Glossary

ancestry   The line of people in your family who lived long before you.

attract   To cause someone to do or like something.

Celts   A group of people from ancient Britain and other parts of western Europe.

climate change   Change in Earth's weather caused by human activity.

festival   A time or event set aside to celebrate.

invade   To enter a country to take control by military force.

represent   To act officially for someone or something.

traditional   Having to do with the ways of doing things in a culture that are passed down from parents to children. Also, following what has been done for a long time.

Find Out More

Books

Cantor, Rachel Anne. *Austria*. Minneapolis, MN:
    Bearport Publishing, 2018.
Dufresne, Emilie. *Austria*. King's Lynn, UK: BookLife,
    2018.

Website

Britannica Kids: Austria

kids.britannica.com/kids/article/Austria/345640
The Britannica Kids page about Austria has facts
about its history, geography, plant and animal life,
and economy.

Video

A Taste of Austria

www.youtube.com/watch?v=SJNgDAx85aI
This video gives viewers a tour of Austria in less than
3 minutes!

Index

About the Author

Kaitlin Scirri is the author of several books for children and teens. She holds a bachelor's degree in writing from the State University of New York at Buffalo State. Other titles by Scirri include *Property Rights, How Facebook Changed the World*, and *Misty Copeland: Ballet Dancer.*